The Best Country Songs Ever

HL HAL LEONARD PUBLISHING CORPORATION

Home Office:
960 East Mark Street
Winona MN 55987

National Sales Office:
8112 West Bluemound Road
Milwaukee WI 53213

ALWAYS ON MY MIND

Words and Music by
WAYNE THOMPSON, MARK JAMES and
JOHNNY CHRISTOPHER

(HEY, WON'T YOU PLAY)
ANOTHER SOMEBODY DONE SOMEBODY WRONG SONG

Words and Music by LARRY BUTLER
and CHIPS MOMAN

Freely

It's lone-ly out to-night and the feel-in' just got right for a

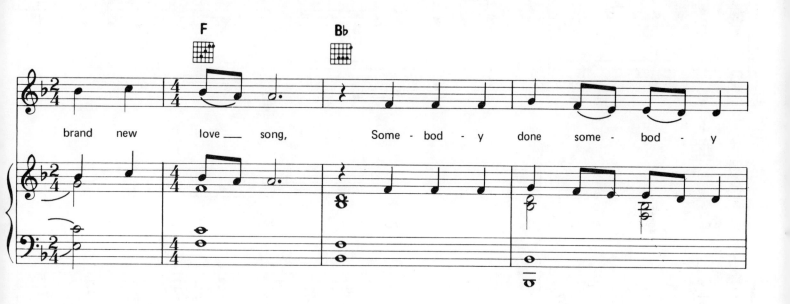

brand new love ___ song, Some-bod - y done some-bod - y

wrong song. Hey won't you play an-oth - er

ANY DAY NOW

Words and Music by BOB HILLIARD
and BURT F. BACHARACH

BEHIND CLOSED DOORS

Words & Music by KENNY O'DELL

Moderately

mf

Verse

My ba-by makes me proud, Lord, don't she make— me proud.

She nev-er makes a scene by hang-in' all o-ver me in a crowd, — 'Cause

Verse

2. (My) baby makes me smile, Lord, don't she make me smile.
   She's never far away or too tired to say I want you.
   She's always a lady, just like a lady should be
   But when they turn out the lights, she's still a baby to me. **(Chorus)**

ANY TIME

Words and Music by
HERBERT HAPPY LAWSON

15

BABY I LIED

Words and Music by RAFE VANHOY,
RORY BOURKE and DEBORAH ALLEN

BUSTED

Words and Music by HARLAN HOWARD

CHARLOTTE'S WEB

Words and Music by JOHN DURRILL,
CLIFF CROFFORD and SNUFF GARRETT

COULD I HAVE THIS DANCE

Words and Music by WAYLAND HOLYFIELD
and BOB HOUSE

I'll al - ways re - mem - ber the song they were play - ing, the
al - ways re - mem - ber that mag - ic mo - ment, when

first time_____ we danced and I knew.   As we
I held_____ you close to me.   As

CRYING IN THE CHAPEL

Slowly, with expression

Words and Music by
ARTIE GLENN

Chorus

1. You saw me Cry-ing In The Chap-el,_____ The tears I shed were tears of
(2. Ev-'ry sin-ner looks for) some-thing_____ That will put his heart at

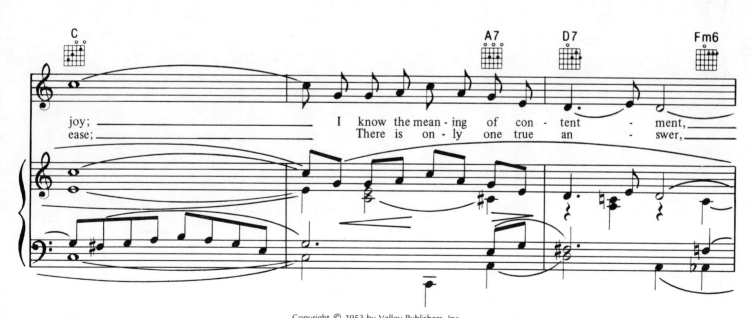

joy;_____ I know the mean-ing of con-tent____ment,_____
ease;_____ There is on-ly one true an____swer,_____

CRAZY

Words and Music by WILLIE NELSON

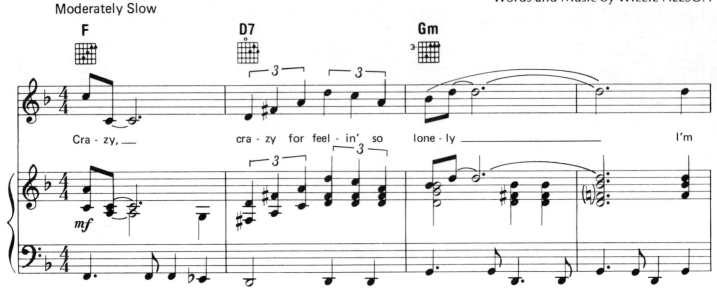

Cra - zy, __ cra - zy for feel - in' so lone - ly __ I'm

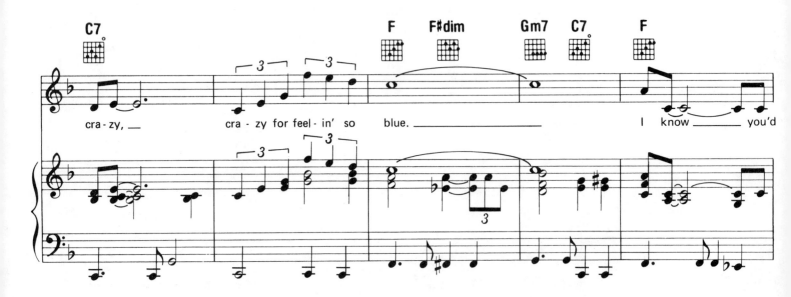

cra - zy, __ cra - zy for feel - in' so blue. __ I know __ you'd

love me as long as you want - ed, __ and then some - day __ you'd leave me for some - bod - y

CRYSTAL CHANDELIERS

Words and Music by TED HARRIS

With movement

All the crys-tal chan-de-liers light up the paint-ings on your wall

The mar-ble stat-u-ettes __ are __ stand-ing state-ly in the

hall __ but will the time-ly crowd __ that has you laugh-ing loud __ help you

34

DADDY DON'T YOU WALK SO FAST

Words and Music by
PETER CALLANDER and GEOFF STEPHENS

DADDY SANG BASS

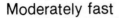

Words and Music by CARL PERKINS

Moderately fast

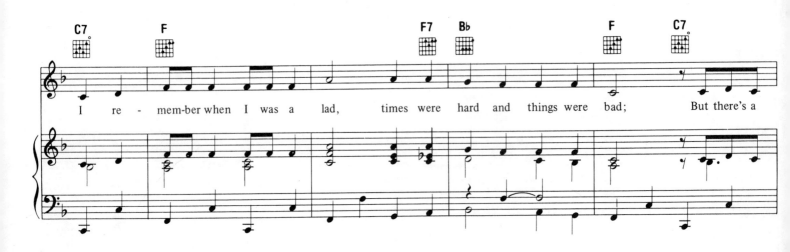

I re-mem-ber when I was a lad, times were hard and things were bad; But there's a

sil-ver lin-ing be-hind ev-'ry cloud._____ Just poor peo-ple that's all we

D-I-V-O-R-C-E

Words and Music by
BOBBY BRADDOCK & CURLY PUTMAN

DETROIT CITY

Words and Music by DANNY DILL
and MEL TILLIS

Hard-Driving rhythm

Last night I went to sleep in De-troit Cit-y and I
Home folks think I'm big in De-troit Cit-y,   from the

dreamed a-bout the cot-ton fields and home; I dreamed a-bout my
let-ters that I write they think I'm fine. But by day I make the

moth-er, dear old pa-pa, sis-ter and broth-er and I dreamed a-bout the
cars, by night I make the bars; if on-ly they could

To Coda

DON'T CHEAT IN OUR HOME TOWN

Words and Music by RAY PENNINGTON
and ROY MARCUM

To - night my heart is beat-ing low,___ and my head is

bowed.___ You've been seen___ with my best friend___ on the

oth - er side of town.___ I don't mind this wait-ing; don't

MAMA'S NEVER SEEN THOSE EYES

Words and Music by J.L. WALLACE
and TERRY SKINNER

Ma-ma says I should-n't be go - in' with you,___ Ma - ma says she knows
Ma-ma says I should-n't let you steal a kiss,___ Ma - ma says it just___ ain't

best. You'll take my heart___ and break___ it in two, 'cause you're just like all___ the rest.___
right. she don't know___ that I can't___ re - sist with the moon so big___ and bright.___

FUNNY HOW TIME SLIPS AWAY

Words and Music by WILLIE NELSON

GOD BLESS THE U.S.A.

Words and Music by LEE GREENWOOD

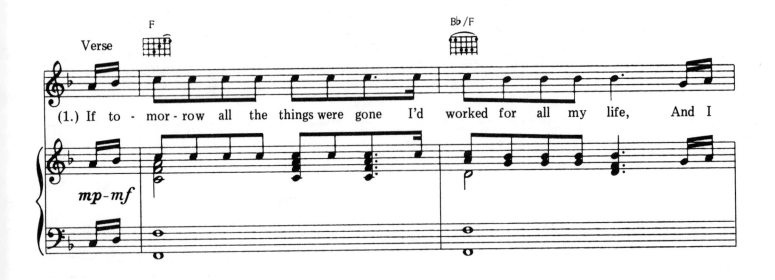

(1.) If to - mor - row all the things were gone I'd worked for all my life, And I

had to start a - gain ____ with just my chil - dren and my wife. I'd

Chorus

GREEN GREEN GRASS OF HOME

Words and Music by CURLY PUTMAN

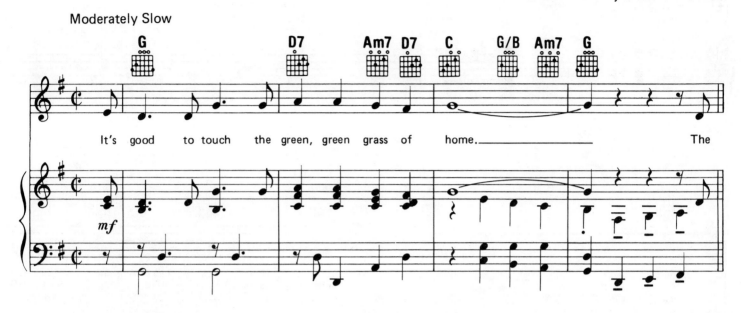

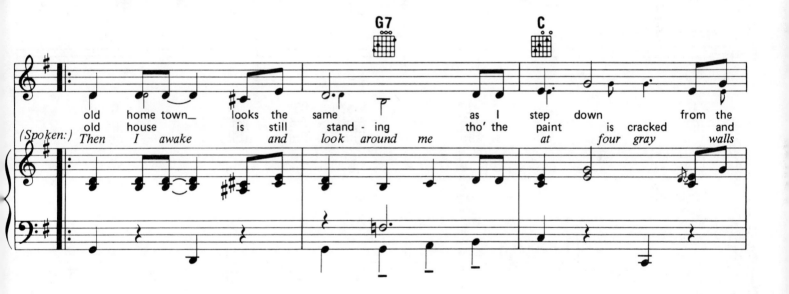

GOOD HEARTED WOMAN

Words and Music by WAYLON JENNINGS
and WILLIE NELSON

A long time for - got - ten, are dreams that just
He likes the night life, the bright lights and

fell by___ the way.
good - tim - in' friends.

And the good life he prom - ised ain't what she's
When the par - ty's all o - ver she'll wel - come

Through tear - drops and laugh - ter, they'll

pass through this world — hand - in - hand,

a good - heart - ed wom - an lov - in' her good - tim - in'

man.

D.S. and Fade

She's a

HE STOPPED LOVING HER TODAY

Words and Music by
BOBBY BRADDOCK & CURLY PUTMAN

Verse 3:

He kept some letters by his bed, dated 1962.
He had underlined in red every single, "I love you".

Verse 4:

I went to see him just today, oh, but I didn't see no tears;
All dressed up to go away, first time I'd seen him smile in years.
(To Chorus:)

Verse 5: *(Spoken)*

You know, she came to see him one last time.
We all wondered if she would.
And it came running through my mind,
This time he's over her for good. (To Chorus:)

HEARTACHES BY THE NUMBER

By HARLAN HOWARD

HELLO WALLS

Words and Music by WILLIE NELSON

HELP ME MAKE IT THROUGH THE NIGHT

Words and Music by KRIS KRISTOFFERSON

Moderato

HONEY
(Open That Door)

Words and Music by MEL TILLIS

Moderate Country

Hon-ey, _____ Hon-ey, _____

Hon-ey won't you o-pen that door?___ This is your sweet dad-dy don't you love me no more?___ It's

cold out-side, let me sleep on the floor,___ Hon-ey won't you o-pen that door?___

To Coda

I honk-y-tonked_ a-round Dal - las, I got in a po-ker_ game._
I went right down to see ol' Bob,_ I thought he was_ my friend._

But some-bod-y must have been cheat-in', I lost ev'-ry-thing but my
The land-lord said that Bob's not here_ the po-lice done hauled him in_

name. I walked half way to Mem-phis. I fin-al-ly got back home._
I ran right back to lit-tle Hon-ey's house._ I got me a rock-in' chair._

But I'd been bet-ter off where I was_ 'cause
Now Hon-ey if you_ don't o - pen that door_ I'm gon-na

I LOVED 'EM EVERY ONE

Words and Music by
PHIL SAMPSON

Moderately bright

for their charms,— holding me in their arms,— and I

hope they had some fun.

fun.

I FALL TO PIECES

Words and Music by HANK COCHRAN
and HARLAN HOWARD

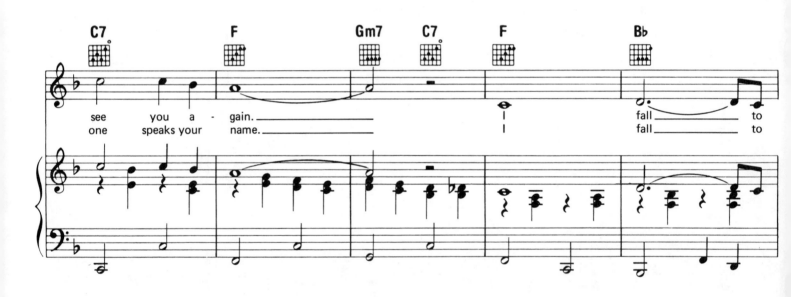

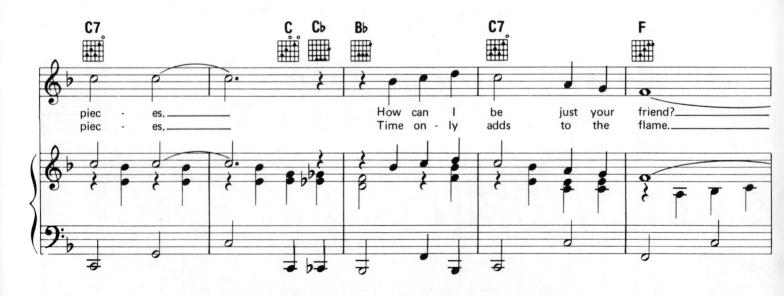

I WAS COUNTRY
WHEN COUNTRY WASN'T COOL

Words and Music by KYE FLEMING
and DENNIS MORGAN

Verse 2:
I remember circling the drive-in,
Pulling up, and turning down George Jones.
I remember when no one was looking,
I was putting peanuts in my coke.
I took a lot of kidding, 'cause I never did fit in;
Now look at everybody trying to be what I was then;
I was country, when country wasn't cool.

Verse 3:
They called us country bumpkins for sticking to our roots;
I'm just glad we're in a country where we're all free to choose;
I was country, when country wasn't cool.

I WISH I WAS EIGHTEEN AGAIN

Words and Music by SONNY THROCKMORTON

off ___ when I heard what that old man had said.
end, ___ and I wish I was eight-een a-gain.

He said, "I'll oh, I wish I was eight-een a-gain, ___

___ and go-ing ___ where I've nev-er been. But

old folks and old oaks stand-ing tall just pre-tend; I

3. (Now,) time turns the pages
   And, oh, life goes so fast;
   The years turn the black hair all gray.
   I talk to some young folks;
   Hey, they don't understand
   The words this old man's got to say.

   (Third ending)

I WOULDN'T HAVE MISSED IT FOR THE WORLD

Words and Music by KYE FLEMING,
DENNIS MORGAN and CHARLES QUILLEN

1. Our paths may nev-er cross a-gain;
2. (see additional lyrics)

may-be my heart will nev-er mend,

but I'm glad for all the good times. You brought me so

Verse 2.
They say that all good things must end.
Love comes and goes just like the wind.
You've got your dreams to follow,
But if I had the chance tomorrow,
You know I'd do it all again.
(To Chorus)

I'M NOT LISA

Words and Music by JESSI COLTER

Moderately Slow

I.O.U.

Words and Music by
AUSTIN ROBERTS & KERRY CHATER

Moderately Slow Ballad

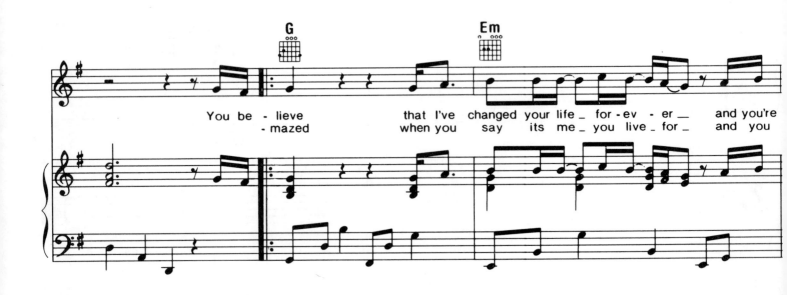

You be - lieve that I've changed your life _ for - ev - er _ and you're
- mazed when you say its me _ you live _ for _ and you

nev - er gon - na find _ an - oth - er some - bod - y like me. _ And you
know that when _ I'm hold - ing, you you're right where you be - long. _ And my

ROCKIN' WITH THE RHYTHM OF THE RAIN

Words and Music by DON SCHLITZ
and BRENT MAHER

MCA MUSIC PUBLISHING

ISLANDS IN THE STREAM

Moderately Slow Rock

Words and Music by BARRY GIBB,
MAURICE GIBB and ROBIN GIBB

Ba - by when I met you there was peace un - known.
I can't live with - out you if the love was gone.

I set out to get you with a fine tooth comb. I was soft in - side___ there___
ev - 'ry - thing is noth - ing if you got no - one and you___ did walk in the night___ slow-

___ was some - thing go - in on.___
- ly lo - sin sight of the real thing.___ But

IT WAS ALMOST LIKE A SONG

Words and Music by ARCHIE JORDAN
and HAL DAVID

IT'S A HEARTACHE

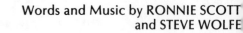

Words and Music by RONNIE SCOTT
and STEVE WOLFE

JAMBALAYA
(ON THE BAYOU)

Moderately

Words and Music by HANK WILLIAMS

3. Settle down far from town, get me a pirogue
And I'll catch all the fish in the bayou
Swap my mon to buy Yvonne what whe need-o
Son of a gun, we'll have big fun on the bayou

KING OF THE ROAD

Words and Music by ROGER MILLER

1,3. Trail - er__ for sale or rent,__ Rooms__ to let__
2. Third box__ car mid - night train,__ Des - ti - na - tion:

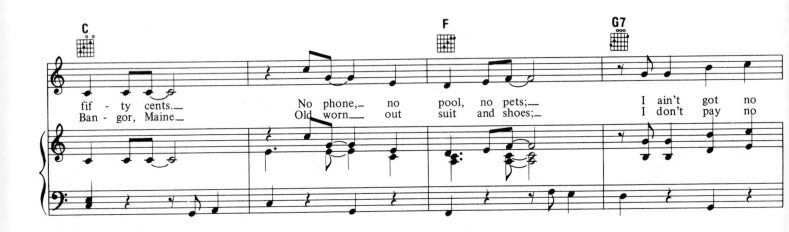

fif - ty cents.__ No phone,__ no pool, no pets;__ I ain't got no
Ban - gor, Maine.__ Old worn__ out suit and shoes;__ I don't pay no

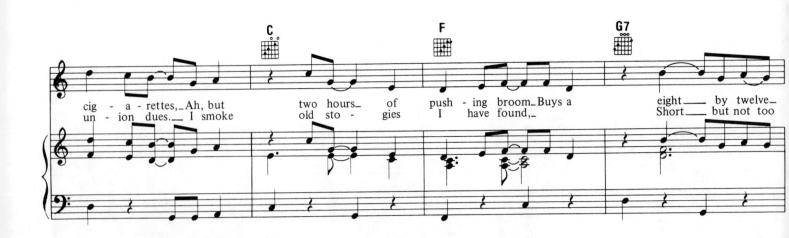

cig - a - rettes, Ah, but two hours__ of push - ing broom Buys a eight__ by twelve
un - ion dues. I smoke old sto - gies I have found,__ Short__ but not too

A LITTLE GOOD NEWS

Words and Music by CHARLIE BLACK,
RORY BOURKE and TOMMY ROCCO

Slow 4

I rolled out this morn-ing the kids had the morn-ing news show on;___ Bry-ant Gum-bel was talk-in' 'bout the fight-ing in

Leb - a - non;___ Some sen - a - tor was squawk-ing 'bout the bad___ e - con-

- o - my.___ It's gon-na get worse you see,___ we need a change in pol - i - cy.___

LITTLE GREEN APPLES

Words and Music by
BOBBY RUSSELL

LUCKENBACH, TEXAS
(Back To The Basics Of Love)

Words and Music by BOBBY EMMONS
and CHIPS MOMAN

128

MAKE THE WORLD GO AWAY

By HANK COCHRAN

MAMMAS DON'T LET YOUR BABIES GROW UP TO BE COWBOYS

Words and Music by ED BRUCE
and PATSY BRUCE

Country Waltz

Mam-mas don't let your ba-bies grow up ___ to be cow-boys.

Don't let 'em pick gui-tars and

drive them old trucks. Make 'em be doc-tors and law-yers and

MIRACLES

Words and Music by ROGER COOK

MY ELUSIVE DREAMS

Words and Music by CURLY PUTMAN
and BILLY SHERRILL

1. You fol-lowed me ___ to Tex-as, You fol-lowed me ___ to U-tah,
2,3 *(See additional lyrics)*

We did-n't find it there so we moved on. ___ You

fol-lowed me ___ to Al-a-bam', Things looked good in Bir-ming-ham,

2. You had my child in Memphis, I heard of work in Nashville,
We didn't find it there so we moved on.
To a small farm in Nebraska to a gold mine in Alaska,
We didn't find it there so we moved on. (Chorus)

3. And now we've left Alaska because there was no gold mine,
But this time only two of us move on.
Now all we have is each other and a little memory to cling to,
And still you won't let me go on alone. (Chorus)

NOBODY LIKES SAD SONGS

Words and Music by WAYLAND HOLYFIELD
and BOB McDILL

PAPER ROSES

Words by JANICE TORRE
Music by FRED SPIELMAN

PERSONALLY

Words and Music by PAUL KELLY

PUT YOUR HAND IN THE HAND

By GENE MacLELLAN

With a beat

RHINESTONE COWBOY

Words and Music by LARRY WEISS

ROCKY TOP

Words and Music by
BOUDLEAUX BRYANT and
FELICE BRYANT

Lively

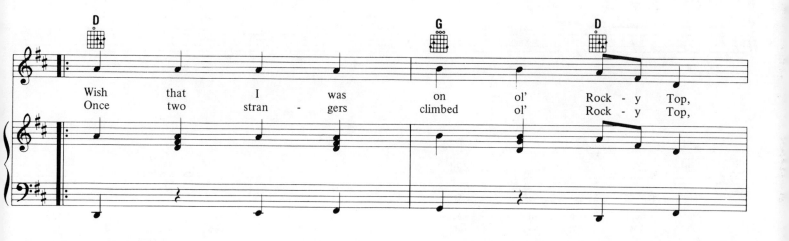

Wish that I was on ol' Rock-y Top,
Once that two stran-gers climbed ol' Rock-y Top,

down in the Tenn-es-see hills; Ain't no smog-gy
look-in' for a moon-shine still; Stran-gers ain't come

Verse 3:
I've had years of cramped-up city life
Trapped like a duck in a pen;
All I know is it's a pity life
Can't be simple again. (Chorus)

RUBY, DON'T TAKE YOUR LOVE TO TOWN

Words and Music
By MEL TILLIS

Don't Take Your Love To Town. For it was -n't me that

started that old cra - zy As - ia war But I was proud to

go and do my pa - tri - ot - ic chores. Oh, I know, Ru - by, that I'm not the

man I used to be, But, Ru - - by,

I still need your com - pa - ny. It's ny. She's

SIXTEEN TONS

Words and Music by
MERLE TRAVIS

Chorus

mind____ that's____ weak____ and a back that's strong. You load
straw - boss____ said____ "Well - a bless my soul." You load
high - toned____ wo - man make me walk the line." You load
night one don't - a get you, then the left one will. You load

Six - teen Tons,

what do you get?____ An - oth - er day old - er and deep - er in debt.____ Saint

Pe - ter, don't you call me 'cause I can't go ____ I owe ____ my soul to the

com - pa - ny store. _____

2. I was
3. I was
4. If you

SMOKY MOUNTAIN RAIN

Words and Music by KYE FLEMING
and DENNIS MORGAN

I thumbed my way from L. A. back to Knox-ville;
I waved a dies-el down out-side a ca-fe;

I found out those bright lights ain't where I be-long.
He said that he was going as far as Gat-lin-burg.

From a phone booth, in the rain, I called to
I climbed up in the cab, All wet and cold and

I can't blame her for let - ting go;____ a wom - an needs some - one warm____

____ to hold.____ I feel the rain run - ning down____ my face;____

I'll find her no mat - ter what it takes.____

D.S. and Fade

SOME DAYS ARE DIAMONDS
(Some Days Are Stone)

Words and Music by DICK FELLER

SOMEBODY'S KNOCKIN'

Words and Music by
ED PENNEY and JERRY GILLESPIE

Moderately

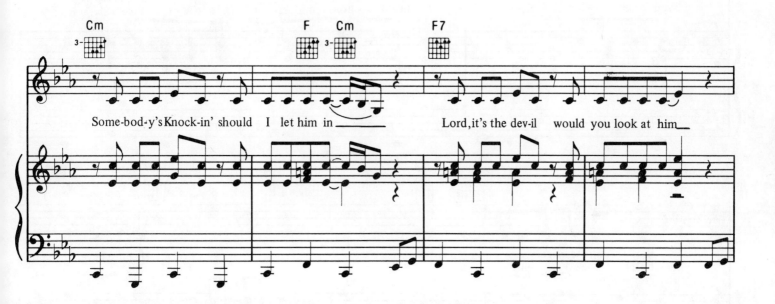

Some-bod-y's Knock-in' should I let him in _____ Lord, it's the dev-il would you look at him _____

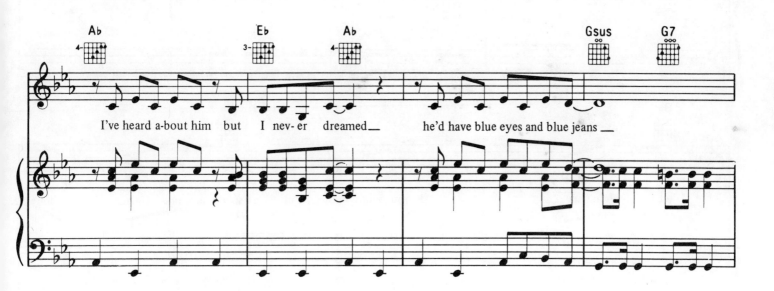

I've heard a-bout him but I nev-er dreamed _____ he'd have blue eyes and blue jeans _____

SOUTHERN NIGHTS

Words and Music by ALLEN TOUSSAINT

SON-OF-A-PREACHER MAN

Words and Music by JOHN HURLEY
and RONNIE WILKINS

1. Jim-my Ray was a preach-er's son when his dad-dy would vis-it he'd come a-long.
2. Be-in' good is-n't al-ways eas-y no mat-ter how I try.

When they gath-ered 'round the par-lor talk-in' cous-in Jim-my would take me walk-in'
When he start-ed sweet talk-in' to me he'd come 'n tell me ev-'ry-thing is al-right;

out thru the back yard we'd go walk-in', And then he'd look in-to my eyes,
kiss and tell me ev-'ry-thing is al-right, And "Can I sneak a-way a-gain to-night."

Lord knows, to my sur-prise, The on-ly one who could ev-er reach me

was the son - of - a preach-er man; The on-ly boy who could ev-er teach me

was the son - of - a preach-er man, yes he was, he was.— Ooh.

How well I re-mem-ber the look that was in his eyes,— Steal-in' kiss-es from me

STAND BY ME

Words and Music by BEN E. KING,
MIKE STOLLER and JERRY LEIBER

STAND BY YOUR MAN

Words and Music by TAMMY WYNETTE and
BILLY SHERRILL

Some - times___ it's hard___ to be a wo - man___
But if___ you love him___ you'll for - give him,___

giv - ing all your love to just
e - ven though he's hard to un - der-

one man.___
stand.___

You'll have___
And if___ you

SWINGIN'

Words and Music by JOHN DAVID ANDERSON
and LIONEL A. DELMORE

1. There's _____ a lit-tle girl in our neigh-bor-hood. Her
2.3. (See additional lyrics)

name is Char-lotte John-son, and she's real-ly look-ing good. I had to go and see her, so I

called her on the phone. I walked o-ver to her house,___ and this was go-in' on: 2. Her

Verse 2.
Her brother was on the sofa
Eatin' chocolate pie.
Her mama was in the kitchen
Cuttin' chicken up to fry.
Her daddy was in the backyard
Rollin' up a garden hose.
I was on the porch with Charlotte
Feelin' love down to my toes,
And we was swingin'. *(To Chorus:)*

Verse 3.
Now Charlotte, she's a darlin';
She's the apple of my eye.
When I'm on the swing with her
It makes me almost high.
And Charlotte is my lover,
And she has been since the spring.
I just can't believe it started
On her front porch in the swing. *(To Chorus:)*

TALK TO ME

Words and Music by JOE SENECA

THE TIP OF MY FINGERS

Words and Music by BILL ANDERSON

THROUGH THE YEARS

Words and Music by
STEVE DORFF and MARTY PANZER

195

TULSA TIME

Words and Music by DANNY FLOWERS

born to just walk the line.
went on back to Tul - sa time.

Liv - in' on Tul - sa time.
Liv - in' on Tul - sa time.
Liv - in' on Tul - sa time.
Liv - in' on Tul - sa time.

Well, you know I been thru it when I set my watch back to it,
Gon - na set my watch back to it, cause you know I've been thru it,

Liv - in' on Tul - sa time.

Well,

D.S. and Fade

WALKING THE FLOOR OVER YOU

Words and Music by
ERNEST TUBB

Swingy tempo

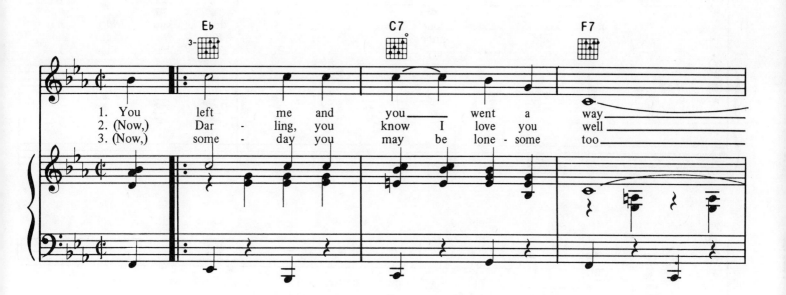

1. You left me and you_____ went a way_____
2. (Now,) Dar - ling, you know I love you well_____
3. (Now,) some - day you may be lone - some too_____

You said that you'd be back in just a day_____
Love you more than I can ev - er tell_____
Walk - ing the floor is good for you_____

WALKING IN THE SUNSHINE

Words and Music by ROGER MILLER

WELCOME TO MY WORLD

By RAY WINKLER
and JOHN HATHCOCK

key to this world of mine, _____ I'll be wait-ing

here _____ with my arms un - furled _____ Wait - ing just for

you, _____ Wel - come to my world. _____

Wel - come to my world. _____

WHAT'S FOREVER FOR

Words and Music by RAFE VANHOY

WHAT A DIFFERENCE YOU'VE MADE IN MY LIFE

Words and Music by ARCHIE JORDAN

What a dif - 'frence you've made ___ in my life; ___ what a dif - 'frence you've made ___ in my life.
change you have made ___ in my heart; ___ what a change you have made in my heart. ___

___ You're my sun - shine day ___ and night. ___ Oh what a
___ You re - placed all the bro - ken parts. ___ Oh what a

dif - 'frence you've made ___ in my life. ___
change you have made ___ in my

215

YOU DON'T KNOW ME

Words and Music by
CINDY WALKER and EDDY ARNOLD

YOU LOOK SO GOOD IN LOVE

Words and Music by KERRY CHATER,
RORY BOURKE and GLEN BALLARD

YOU PUT THE BEAT IN MY HEART

Words and Music by DON PFRIMMER
and RICK GILES

Fast Country Rock beat

love ne-ver real-ly moved in me 'til you put the beat in my

heart. I

thought I heard some-one knock-in', or foot-steps in the hall, or

may-be it was a branch blow-in' on the win-dow pane. But

Bm

you were lay-in' be-side___ me,___ Soft___ as the morn-in' light.___ I knew that the

F#m/A

G6 ... **A** ... **Bm**

D.S. al Coda

sound I was hear-in'___ now start-ed in your arms___ that night.

CODA **Bm**

Put the beat in my heart.___ Ooh

G6 ... **A** ... **Bm**

Repeat and Fade

You,_____ you put the beat in my heart.___ Don't_ you_ know_that?_

YOU NEEDED ME

Words and Music by RANDY GOODRUM

WHY NOT ME

Medium Country

Words and Music by HARLAN HOWARD,
SONNY THROCKMORTON and BRENT MAHER

YOU'RE MY BEST FRIEND

Words and Music by WAYLAND HOLYFIELD

YOUR CHEATIN' HEART

Words and Music by HANK WILLIAMS